A gift for:

From:

If you love this book...
you will probably want to know how to find other
Helen Exley®LONDON gifts like it. They're all listed on

www.helenexley.com

Helen Exley, who created Mothers & Daughters, lived thousands of miles
from her mother. She phoned her every other day.
"I knew everything in her life, and she was the same with me – she even knew
what the weather was like here. She meant the world to me.
That's why I love these quotes. They say everything we'd all like to say
to someone who is so central, so vital to our life."

OTHER BOOKS IN THE SERIES

For my Granddaughter 365 365 Happy Days! For my Sister 365

The Secrets of Happiness 365 For my Daughter 365 Friendship 365

Mothers&Daughters

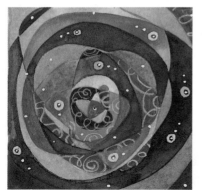

No relationship is as highly charged as that between mother and daughter, or as riddled with expectations that could, like a landmine, detonate with a single misstep, a solitary stray word that, without warning, wounds or enrages. And no relationship is as bursting with possibilities of goodwill and understanding.

VICTORIA SECUNDA

EDITED BY HELEN EXLEY
ILLUSTRATIONS BY JULIETTE CLARKE

Published in 2017 and 2021 by Helen Exley ® LONDON in Great Britain.
Design, selection and arrangement are all © Helen Exley Creative Ltd 2017, 2021.
All the words by Pam Brown, Fatima Boutros, Samantha Armstrong, Pamela Dugdale, Odile Dormeuil,
Annelou Dupuis, Helen M. Exley, Lisette Favier, Mathilde Forestier, Mathilde and Sébastien Forestier,
Charlotte Gray, Charlotte Granier, Lisa Scully O'Grady, Linda Macfarlane, Stuart and Linda Macfarlane,
Siân E. Morgan, Sian Morgan, Lisa Rochambeau-La Pierre, Caroline Ramuz,
Helen Thomson are all copyright © Helen Exley Creative Ltd 2017, 2021.

ISBN 978-1-78485-084-5

12   11   10   9   8   7   6   5   4   3

Helen Exley ® LONDON
16 Chalk Hill, Watford, Herts WD19 4BG, UK
www.helenexley.com

JANUARY 2

Every ounce of love a mother gives to her child nourishes, reinforces, encourages, and teaches not only her child but herself.

ALEXANDRA STODDARD

DECEMBER · 31

You have thoughts and adventures I shall never share.
I stand and look at you and am closer to you than anything else
I know about. You are a part of me which is completely free.

LIV ULLMANN, B. 1939

JULY 3

We two enhance each other's being.

PAMELA DUGDALE

Mothers&Daughters

Spring, the birth of nature; soft air
filled with the promise of warmth,
sun speckling the ground and a new
young mother with her baby daughter
soothed and asleep in her arms
under a tree.
What nicer piece of life?

JANE-LOUISE MIDDLETON

Mothers&Daughters

My first thought of you
is of overwhelming, overflowing love.
An unconditional love, born out of your being my firstborn,
my vulnerable, disabled daughter.

WENDY

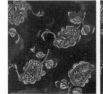

Mothers&Daughters

From the moment I saw you I knew
that we were meant to do great things in life, together.
I love you as much as any mother could love her child.

JENNIFER

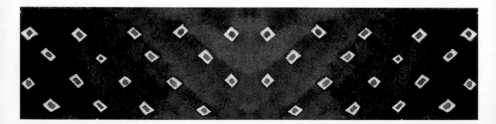

JULY 5

Every now and again
one needs a Day Out
with Mum. Small, silly
extravagances.
Shoes off in the train.

CHARLOTTE GRAY

Mothers&Daughters

I held your
tiny hand
and suddenly
miracles
seemed possible.

MATHILDE FORESTIER

JULY 6

LITTLE GIRL
I will buy you a house
If you do not cry,
A house, little girl,
As big as the sky.

I will furnish the house
For you and for me,
With walnuts
Fresh from the tree.

ARABIAN NURSERY RHYME

Mothers&Daughters

Mothers who admire their daughters
are the luckiest women in the world.
Thank you for making me the luckiest of lucky.

LINDA MACFARLANE, B. 1953

Mothers&Daughters

Thank you for all the times when I thought
I didn't need you, but you were there anyway to give me
a helping hand when things went terribly wrong.

LISA SCULLY-O'GRADY

Mothers&Daughters

Patterns of childhood changed overnight as in a shaken kaleidoscope and you were left wondering if anything you ever said or did or tried for had any part in her making. But sometimes, unexpectedly, you'll hear her say something with firm conviction – and they are your words and it is your voice.

PAM BROWN 1928 – 2014

Mothers&Daughters

Do you remember the rituals?
The small solemnities that make
most ordinary things special.
A little splash of coffee in my milk.
Staying up an extra hour.
Crossing the road without holding hands.
Rituals of passage.
A gentling into growing.

PAMELA DUGDALE

JUNE 27

Thank you for giving me the things I needed
to be a strong mother – your love and support.

LARAMIE

Mothers&Daughters

As a girl reaches her thirties
her love for her mother deepens –
for it is then that she realises
that they both share the same faults!

LINDA MACFARLANE, B. 1953

Mothers&Daughters

Ever since you first came into my life
there always seems to be some exciting news.
And each day with you seems to bring anticipation
and excitement, something more to discover.
I never know what the day will bring.
That's the beauty of having a daughter.

SIÂN E. MORGAN, B. 1973

Mothers&Daughters

Thank you Mum
for laying the plates for supper around the cardboard castle
that filled the table. It had taken days to build.
So we talked around turrets and passed the salt
through the portcullis. And planned a dungeon.

ODILE DORMEUIL

Mothers&Daughters

Last night I was in pain,
and made a sort of moan. She was lying by me,
apparently asleep; but as if her gentle instinct
of love prompted her even then,
she pressed to me, saying, "Kiss, Mama."
These are trifles, but how very precious
may the remembrance of them become....

MRS ELIZABETH GASKELL 1810 – 1865

Mothers&Daughters

My mother is like a tall fruit tree because she is strong, tall and big. My mother is like morning because she is like sunshine coming up. My mother is like a mango because she is sweet. My mother is like an armchair because she is cosy and warm.

TANIA TSIMABA BUEYA, AGE 8

JUNE 24

Forgive me the times
I was aggravating
and thoughtless and stupid.
Thank you for your
patience and your love.

PAMELA DUGDALE

Mothers&Daughters

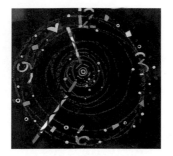

No one but a mother can know the sheer relief
on a night of storm to hear a knock and find her daughter
safely on the doorstep.

PAM BROWN 1928 – 2014

Mothers&Daughters

Mothers and daughters are part of each other's consciousness, in different degrees and in a different way, but still with the mutual sense of something which has always been there.

EDITH WHARTON 1862 – 1937

Mothers&Daughters

I love you and have always loved you. To the best of my ability, with the work of my body, the limits of my mind. I have tried to give you love, shelter, and food. I have tried to give you fun and laughter.

AUTHOR UNKNOWN

Mothers&Daughters

I miss her all the time.
Her voice, her smile, her love, her wisdom.
But I feel a part of her has merged with me.
I know what she'd think: "Go for it..."
And she's given me the freedom to do just that.

CAROLE STONE

Mothers&Daughters

And she sings, long notes
from the belly or the throat,
Her legs kick her feet up
to her nose,
She rests – laid still like
a large rose.
She is our child...

JENNIFER ARMITAGE

When her daughter needs help, mountains
and miles cannot hold back a mother.

LINDA MACFARLANE, B. 1953

Mothers&Daughters

Sooner or later
a woman will see
that her hands
have changed into
her mother's.

PAMELA DUGDALE

Mothers & Daughters

A girl's love for her mother
is unique. It is not shown
in exaggerated gestures and
theatrical displays. It is a deep,
quiet love which,
even when unspoken,
is as strong as the forces of nature
that lock the Earth and Moon.

LISETTE FAVIER

Mothers&Daughters

She is mine, part of me.
If she hurts, I hurt, if she is unhappy,
I am unhappy and if she triumphs,
so do I.

PENNY VINCENZI, B. 1939

JUNE 19

Mothers start our lives.
They cast on our existence…
They give us the basic patterns. But the good ones…
hand over the needles after a while, and say:
"There's the world, love. Choose yourself some new shades,
some new patterns. Make yourself a life."

PAM BROWN 1928 – 2014

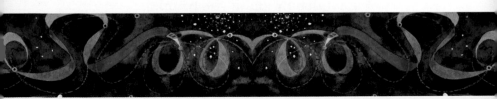

JULY 17

You know, Jodie, I think most of the things I value or have
helped me grow have had elements of pain or hard work.
I want to share this with you so you don't miss out
on good things just because they are hard.

SUSAN

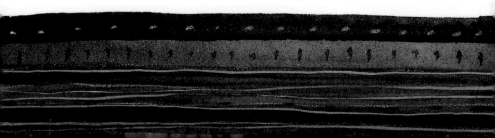

Mothers&Daughters

JUNE 18

When the mother-daughter relationship is in good
working order, it is a rock of strength in an age of uncertainties.
Even when rushing eddies threaten, its foundations stay firm
and the rock, apparently submerged for good,
reappears to assert its importance once more.

RACHEL BILLINGTON, B. 1942

JULY 18

I am always with you,
as we know miles
mean nothing to you and I.
We always live
in one another's hearts.

JUNE HIRD

I already begin to be devoured with expectation.
I hope for no consolation but from your letters and yet
I know they will only make me sigh still more deeply.
In short, my dear child, I live but for you.

MADAME DE SÉVIGNÉ 1626 – 1696

Mothers&Daughters

A daughter is a little person who comes into your world
and takes over your life.

LISETTE FAVIER

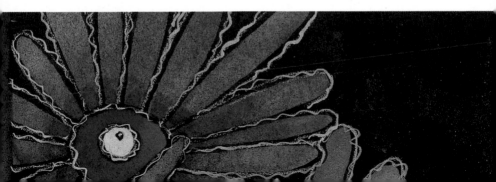

Mothers & Daughters

Every mother...

has a drawer full of extraordinary gifts

donated by her daughters

over a lifetime. All pristine. All treasured.

PAM BROWN 1928 – 2014

Mothers&Daughters

Do you remember – winter mornings,
dark and cold and rustling?
The first day away, walking to a shining sea
and the sound of gulls?
Lopsided birthday cakes?
Walks through spring woods?
I do, I do.

PAM BROWN 1928 – 2014

JUNE 15

I needed someone
to talk to.
Someone to listen.
Someone to try
to understand.
And it has always
been you.

ARLOTTE GRAY

Mothers&Daughters

You pause, just ready to grow up.
Your smile – I will be a woman like you, my smile says,
you are pure delight. In that flash of love and homage
we know it is sweet to be female.

CHRISTINE CRAIG

JUNE 14

... think of our beautiful three weeks at the seashore –
of sunrise, and when we walked barefoot along the beach...
and when we read books together.
We had so many beautiful things together, my child,
and you must experience all of them over again,
and much more besides...

ROSE SCHOSINGER 1907 – 1943

JULY 22

You are becoming a young woman and there is so much I want to say. It is hard to find the words or time in our everyday life to tell you all the things I want you to know. I can only hope that we continue to be friends as well as family so that we will always openly communicate.

LINDA

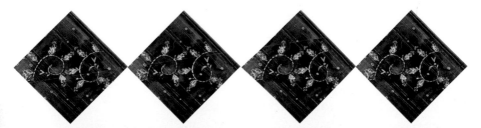

Mothers&Daughters

JUNE 13

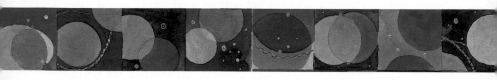

*Mothers and daughters
share a history, genes, love...
and if they are very lucky...
shoes.*

STUART & LINDA MACFARLANE

JULY 23

I think of you as my best investment,
my best work, my best achievement,
the very best thing I ever did.

SIÂN E. MORGAN, B. 1973

JUNE 12

Give her a good start.

Wish her well.

And let her go.

She'll be back.

Stand by with hugs.

PAMELA DUGDALE

Mothers&Daughters

The truth is that when
one woman gives birth
to another,
to someone who is like her,
they are linked together
for life.

NANCY FRIDAY, B. 1933

What do girls
do who haven't any mothers
to help them
through their troubles?

LOUISA MAY ALCOTT
1832 – 1888

Mothers&Daughters

I keep an album of photographs of you – as if I could
hold on to all the different yous – the baby, the toddler,
the schoolgirl, the teenager...
you are all of them – and every time I see you I think
"This is the best time."

PAM BROWN 1928 – 2014

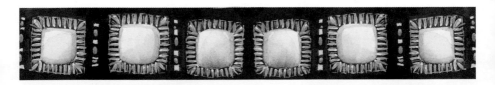

Mothers & Daughters

I become her sidekick, her buddy, her duenna,
her walking credit card. I resent it, yet I also love it more
than anything. She fills me up with feeling as no one can.

ERICA JONG, B. 1942

Mothers&Daughters

...women pass on from mother to daughter a heredity
far more real than anything shown on the traditionally male
genealogical table. It expresses itself at an everyday level
of practical caring and at a deeper level of emotional
self-identification and wholeness. But, above all, it is
a teacher of love – the first teacher and the most important,
from which all other love stems.

RACHEL BILLINGTON, B. 1942

JUNE 9

I never thought
I could love so much
or hurt so badly
for another person.

JENNIFER

JULY 27

I talk to you as a mother, a sister,
and your number one girlfriend.
I am proud of you for all
the things that you are.
I wish I could physically be
with you on your journey of life;
I know you'll be phenomenal.

KARLA

Mothers&Daughters

Everyone needs a mother to cheer
when things go right. It's good to have the applause of friends,
family and colleagues – but one looks above their heads,
to make sure your mother is clapping!

PAM BROWN 1928 – 2014

Mothers & Daughters

A mother knows she's a success when her daughter asks to borrow her new coat.

STUART & LINDA MACFARLANE

Mothers&Daughters

But I like to remember the two
in the lamp lit evenings by the cottage fire,
during the first of those new-born weeks,
the child feeding at the breast, the sleepy adjusting
fingers, the bunting mouth, the little grunts
of concentration and bliss. I don't think
I've ever seen them since in such a state
of single-minded agreement, so quietly
immersed in their shared purposes.

LAURIE LEE 1914 – 1997

JULY 29

Thank you for your patience
– when I've been cantankerous,
moody, sulky, dull,
when I've been muddled,
when I've been distracted.
Thank you for waiting for me to come around.
Bringing light into the gloom.
Welcoming me home.

ODILE DORMEUIL

Mothers&Daughters

A mother is a girl's
number one fan.
Whether she comes last in a race
or is singing out of tune,
mum will always be there
to impartially assure her
that she is the greatest.

LISETTE FAVIER

Mothers&Daughters

JULY 30

I feel your arms holding me safe,
even with thousands of miles between us.

PAM BROWN 1928 – 2014

Mothers&Daughters

My courage,
my growing strength and happiness.
They've been the best thank you
I could have given you.

HELEN M. EXLEY

Mothers&Daughters

Wherever you are – in city street
or in the hush and glimmer
of a summer wood –
our love is with you.
It shines in the quiet pool.
It wheels above you
in the flight of swallows.

CHARLOTTE GRAY

Mothers&Daughters

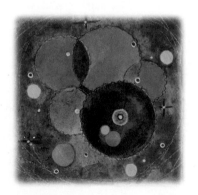

Grown daughters
nag a bit but,
they say,
It's Only For Your Own Good.

PAMELA DUGDALE

Mothers&Daughters

The most vivid memories
of my youth are linked
with my mother's kitchen,
coming home to the warmth
of a log fire and good food,
lovingly prepared.

MARGARET FULTON

Mothers&Daughters

I want to thank my mother
for working and always paying for my piano lessons
before she paid the Bank of America loan
or bought the groceries
or had our old rattling Ford repaired.

DIANE WAKOSKI, B. 1937

Mothers&Daughters

I wanted to change the world overnight, to make it a safer, easier, better place for this miniature woman, this receptacle of all my dreams and aspirations... this extension of myself.

MICHELE GUINNESS

Mothers&Daughters

A mother and daughter
may stop talking
to each other
but they can never
stop loving each other.

LINDA MACFARLANE, B. 1953

Mothers&Daughters

Mothers learn very early
that daughters will do
as daughters do –
and all a mother can do
is stand by
to pick up the pieces.

PAMELA DUGDALE

Mothers&Daughters

On a daily basis,
I recognize the many ways we are alike:
the shape of our faces, the strength of our legs,
our stubbornness.
Our bond is forever a very special one.

KATHRYN

Mothers&Daughters

I have been wondering if it was as hard for you to go out into the world as it was for me to have you go... But tell me all your thoughts and dreams and plans, your worries and trials, and we will talk them over as two comrades...

FLORENCE WENDEROTH SAUNDERS, B. 1926

Mothers&Daughters

Anything that happens, you can confide in Mama.
Nothing's too bad to tell Mama. Don't ever tell me a lie.
It's not necessary, because Mama will understand.

NANNY JAMES LOGAN DELANY

Mothers & Daughters

My mother wanted me
to be her wings,
to fly as she never quite
had the courage to do.
I love her for that.
I love the fact that she
wanted to give birth
to her own wings.

ERICA JONG, B. 1942

MAY 30

It is a lifetime trust.

It has made

all the difference,

knowing you are there

always, always.

HANNAH KLEIN

Mothers&Daughters

Nothing looks as lonely as your mom
before she sees you coming up the platform.

PAM BROWN 1928 – 2014

Mothers&Daughters

Emily is wonderful: she's like the sun,
she comes out and everyone starts feeling warmer.

JILLY COOPER, B. 1937

AUGUST 7

You taught me to soar,
to rise high above
the worries of life.
You taught me how to fly,
and then set me free.

LINDA MACFARLANE, B. 1953

MAY 28

"See, no dragons
underneath the bed.
Sleep now." you said.
"Safe and sound till morning -
I'm never far away."
And so I drifted into sleep,
wrapped in your love.

PAM BROWN 1928 – 2014

Mothers&Daughters

Anything I have I'd give to you,
to thank you. But nothing could pay you back
for making me feel so special.

HELEN THOMSON

Mothers&Daughters

In those saddest moments, I am reminded
that you're not completely invincible.
Not just yet. And secretly I'm glad that you sometimes,
just sometimes, still need me.

SIÂN E. MORGAN, B. 1973

Mothers&Daughters

Carnal, spiritual, and profound, the bond which unites mothers and daughters is, by nature, indestructible.

VIVIANE ESDERS

MAY 26

When a mother and daughter
have plenty to share,
they can be many miles apart
and yet be close.

SHEILA KITZINGER 1929 – 2015

Mothers&Daughters

She gave you life.
What greater gift could she bestow?
The sky. The stars.
Rivers and waterfalls.
Mountains and meadows.
Music.
Friendship.
Love.

ODILE DORMEUIL

Mothers & Daughters

Whatever happens...
our lives are stitched together by a thread of gold
that cannot change, whatever changes come.

PAM BROWN 1928 – 2014

Mothers&Daughters

If you had never been born this planet would be a little colder,
a little more drab and dull.... you have brought laughter
to my life, and kindliness and caring. Through your eyes
I've discovered wonders from your hands, the gift of friendship.

PAM BROWN 1928 – 2014

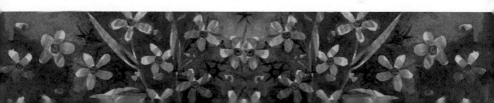

Mothers&Daughters

Once you seemed very old and wise
and indestructible.
How strange to find that now we are contemporaries,
two women, two friends.

ODILE DORMEUIL

I am an onlooker on my daughter's
dance, which I... made possible because
she came through me...
I'm not part of her dance.
Yet whenever she takes a pause
and needs someone to talk to,
I am there. But that special dance
with the child and the future is hers.

LIV ULLMANN, B. 1939

Mothers&Daughters

The baby has learned to smile, and her smiles burst forth like holiday sparklers, lighting our hearts. Joy fills the room. At what are we smiling? We don't know, and we don't care. We are communicating with one another in happiness, and the smiles are the outward display of our delight and our love.

JOAN LOWERY NIXON 1927 – 2003

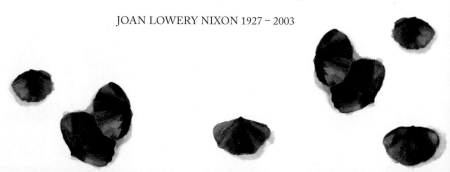

Mothers&Daughters

I have a university degree, a highly paid
job and a fine house. I have achieved
so much in my life – but it has only been
possible because of the many sacrifices
my mother made for me.
Thank you.

LINDA MACFARLANE, B. 1953

Mothers&Daughters

You came third in the 100 metres,
second in the long jump,
but always first in my heart.

LINDA MACFARLANE, B. 1953

Mothers&Daughters

I give you the city, my dearest. The glitter of shop fronts,
the roar of traffic. Palaces and parks. Ducks and pigeons.
Swathes of pictures. Little secret squares and towers to climb.
A river running to the sea.
And you and me.
And ice cream cones for two.

CHARLOTTE GRAY

Mothers&Daughters

How did this happen?
Days ago, you were trailing behind.
Small. Insistent.
My little lass.
And now
here you are, facing me across the café table,
our carrier bags heaped against our feet.
My contemporary.
My friend.

PAMELA DUGDALE

Mothers & Daughters

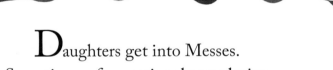

Daughters get into Messes.
Sometimes of exceptional complexity.
And Mothers pull themselves together
and Think.
Sadly, they often fail to find solutions.
All they can do is be there.

PAM BROWN 1928 – 2014

MAY 20

I recall a time in my life during which I was in
severe emotional pain. One morning I woke up to find
my thirteen-year-old daughter sleeping on the floor beside my bed.
When I questioned her about this she quietly told me
that she wanted to be near me because she knew I was hurting…

BARBARA THOMAS

AUGUST 16

Nothing could give me greater happiness than when I hear her throaty little laugh or see her clapping her hands in delight.

ANNA PASTERNAK

MAY 19

...it was my daughter who often
seemed most meaningful
in my struggle for my lost Self.
She was my little Echo,
my "mirror,"
the answer to a mother's dreams.

COLETTE DOWLING, B. 1938

Mothers & Daughters

When the nurse brought my baby in,
I looked into her face and saw myself –
her eyes, her skin, her expressions, her spirit...
From that moment on my heart was all hers.
I was terrified, elated, proud, and complete...
all at once... On that day... we began our
wonderful duet, a blend of heart, mind,
and soul that continues to this day.

NAOMI JUDD, B. 1946

Mothers&Daughters

When my mother and I are in the same room
we work magic on each other:
I grow impossibly cheerful and am guilty of reimagined naiveté
and other indulgent stunts, and my mother's sad,
helpless dithering becomes a song of succour.

CAROL SHIELDS

Mothers&Daughters

The best thing you can do is believe in yourself.

Don't be afraid to try.

Don't be afraid to fail.

Just try again.

Just dust yourself off and try again…

My love and thoughts go with you.

My first child.

My daughter.

JUDY GREEN HERBSTREIT

Mothers&Daughters

Sales are largely supported
by mothers and daughters
looking for surprises for each other.

PAM BROWN 1928 – 2014

Mothers&Daughters

Catastrophe.
Coffee down my best dress.
Suddenly overdrawn.
Dropped my phone down the loo.
Can't remember where I put my keys.
Who always has a solution?
You. Always you.

PAMELA DUGDALE

Mothers&Daughters

But I did kiss you in the night and chased away
your nightmares; and I made up stories and songs
that made you laugh full and strong, and most times,
I was there for you and recognized, most clearly
that facing you is facing me.

MARGARET SLOAN-HUNTER 1947 – 2004

Mothers & Daughters

She says she hates you and she does.
Wait for a little while until the anger and resentment passes.
Be patient.
One day, some day, she'll turn and smile
And you will find yourselves loving friends, forever.

ODILE DORMEUIL

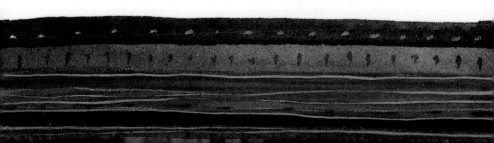

MAY 15

A mother's
ability is to
listen and
to understand.

ODILE DORMEUIL

August 21

A daughter fills the sky with stars –
each one a happy memory.

LINDA MACFARLANE, B. 1953

Mothers&Daughters

MAY 14

My daughter is a Phenomenon, really the most wonderful
Natural Production I ever beheld…

LADY HOLLAND

Mothers&Daughters

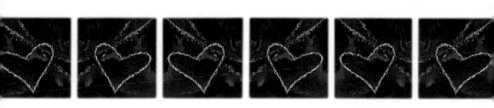

She works hard for a living especially for me and my brothers and we all appreciate it. She is really concerned about her family so she works extra hard.

STEPHANIE JONES, AGE 10

Mothers&Daughters

MAY 13

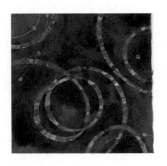

How good it is,
laden with shopping,
to reach the café,
find a table, dump the bags
– and slip off our tightening shoes.
A cup of tea, a buttered bun,
a review of the day's small triumphs.
Mother and daughter,
dearest friends.

PAM BROWN 1928 – 2014

AUGUST 23

To my children:
Never make fun of having to help me
with computer stuff.
I taught you how to use a spoon.

SUE FITZMAURICE

Mothers&Daughters

Motherhood:
A job with long hours, hard labour and no wages –
but the most satisfying job of all.

LINDA MACFARLANE, B. 1953

Mothers & Daughters

August 24

I remember so clearly those things you did
for the very first time...Watching you go to school,
with me feeling proud, anxious and nervous, all at once!...
Your first play when I sat in the audience and whispered
your lines along with you.

SIÂN E. MORGAN, B. 1973

Mothers&Daughters

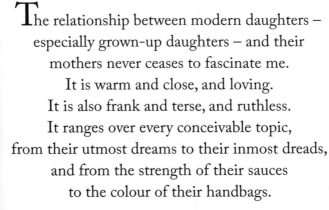

The relationship between modern daughters –
especially grown-up daughters – and their
mothers never ceases to fascinate me.
It is warm and close, and loving.
It is also frank and terse, and ruthless.
It ranges over every conceivable topic,
from their utmost dreams to their inmost dreads,
and from the strength of their sauces
to the colour of their handbags.

GODFREY SMITH

Mothers&Daughters

You are my strength, my treasure and my friend –
the rock that has endured through all the shifting years.
My dear, my dearest mother.
Thank you.

PAM BROWN 1928 – 2014

Mothers&Daughters

"Thank heavens for little girls"…
With pigtails and pony tails, in jeans and party dresses,
climbing trees, reading books,
sucking gobstoppers and turning cartwheels…

MICHELE GUINNESS

Mothers&Daughters

Nobody can divide me from my mother.
Time and distance make no difference to us.

HANNAH KLEIN

MAY 9

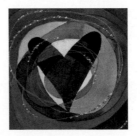

Let us sit here together
and share the sunlight and be happy.

PAMELA DUGDALE

Mothers&Daughters

Your pain
I could not bear for you.
I could not remember
my pain for you.
Only the small life
in my arms -
My girl,
my daughter – you.

BARBARA RENNIE

Mothers&Daughters

Sometimes I stand there, telling you off
for something that I am guilty of myself
(which you are usually very quick to point out).
Only a daughter could point out my flaws
and get away with it!

SIÂN E. MORGAN, B. 1973

Mothers&Daughters

Sometimes, as you lay peacefully sleeping in your crib,
I would gently take your tiny hand in mine
just to share your peace and serenity.

LINDA MACFARLANE, B. 1953

Mothers&Daughters

I gaze at her fine, pink face, glowing
in the window light... Everything glows.
I am aglow with the rapture of the revelation
that she is the most beautiful in the whole
world, my mother. It is an intensely aesthetic
pleasure, experienced, thank goodness,
before the pinched and crabbed world
with its penny-ruler measurements
interposed its decrees.

ADELE WISEMAN 1928 – 1992

Mothers&Daughters

When I hold her exhausted from the day's work
and the disturbed nights, there is a deep relief and pleasure
at finding myself able to give again and again...
I've at last found the good mother within me,
the ability to put someone else's needs before my own.

JEAN RADFORD

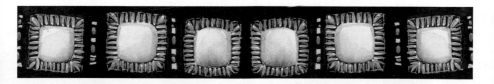

MAY 6

You made me feel I belonged. What a gift!

HELEN M. EXLEY

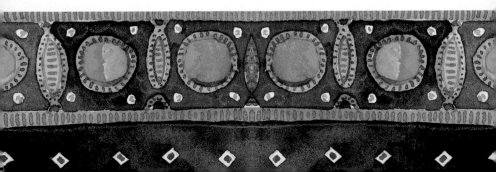

August 30

I carry your picture
in my wallet
and your smile
in my heart.

MATHILDE FORESTIER

Mothers&Daughters

Love is;

Tidying up her bedroom, Putting up with her tantrums,
Coping with idiosyncrasies, Cooking her special treats,
Listening to her ramblings, Because when you were little,
Your mother did these for you.

MATHILDE FORESTIER

Mothers&Daughters

Daughters exasperate mothers.
Mothers exasperate daughters.
But they love each other rotten.

PAM BROWN 1928 – 2014

Mothers&Daughters

Part of us resents forever the fact that we and our mothers
were closer than we can ever be to any other creature.
They gave us freedom – but we sense the hidden bond,
and know it's unbreakable.

PAM BROWN 1928 – 2014

Mothers&Daughters

She cared for me day in, day out during my childhood, driving me here and there, soothed me when I was hurt, worried with me over problems, and set me an example of poise, courage, and gallantry.

MOLLY HASKIN

Mothers&Daughters

When we are sharing a cake
and you cut it in half,
somehow I always end up
with the bigger 'half'.

LINDA MACFARLANE, B. 1953

Mothers&Daughters

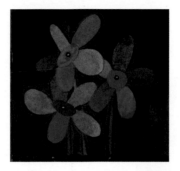

You make me glad to be alive. Thank you.

LINDA MACFARLANE, B. 1953

MAY 2

Before you were born
I loved you
Before you were here
an hour I would die for you.

MAUREEN HAWKINS

Mothers&Daughters

Mothers of daughters are daughters
of mothers and have remained so,
in circles joined to circles, since time began.

SIGNE HAMMER

Mothers&Daughters

When my mother goes somewhere I look for her everywhere.
She loves me more than anyone.
When I can't find her I cry, I trust her she'll never lie.
I can't stay without her. Wherever we walk we're a pair.

HUSNA KHATUN, AGE 11

Mothers&Daughters

Gradually I began to realize that she liked me,
that she had no option to liking me. It was very pleasant
to receive such uncritical love, because it left me free
to bestow love; my kisses were met by small warm rubbery
unrejecting cheeks and soft dovey mumblings of delight.

MARGARET DRABBLE, B. 1939

Mothers&Daughters

We want to please our mothers, emulate them, disgrace them, oblige them, outrage them, and bury ourselves in the mysteries and consolations of their presence.

CAROL SHIELDS

Mothers&Daughters

Dearest Daughter.
One tiny tug will have me
dropping anything
I'm engaged in – you are,
above everything,
the heartbeat of my life.

CHARLOTTE GRAY

Mothers&Daughters

There has never been anything that you have done
that has taken away my unconditional love for you.

AUTHOR UNKNOWN

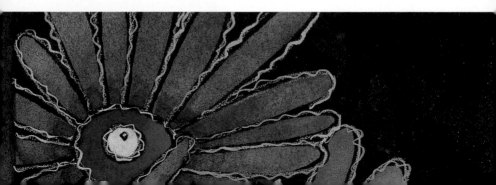

Mothers&Daughters

With mothers and daughters you never really know whose is the initiative. We are so interwoven, so symbiotic, that you cannot always tell the mother from the daughter, the dancer from the dance.

ERICA JONG, B. 1942

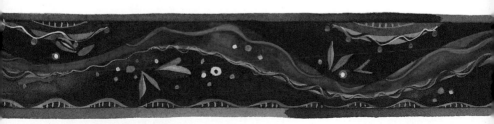

APRIL 28

W̲hen I look into your eyes I feel mine shine with love.

LINDA MACFARLANE, B. 1953

Mothers&Daughters

Sometimes when I'm feeling particularly
useless you give me sound advice –
which I once gave you. It cheers me up no end.
Thanks for keeping an eye on me, love.

PAMELA DUGDALE

Mothers & Daughters

You are here when I spoon cranberries into the cut glass dish,
the footed one, and put the pickles and olives in the flat one.
I feel your presence when I knot a twine trellis for the sweet peas
to climb and when I pick violets and breathe in their fragrance –
the only scent you ever wore.

TESS ENROTH 1925 – 2014

Mothers&Daughters

I was poorly in bed with a fever
and woke from a fretful sleep
to find that you had placed
your teddy beside me
to help me feel better!

LINDA MACFARLANE, B. 1953

Mothers&Daughters

Sometimes mothers scold their daughters
when they are small…"For their own good."
Time changes things. And daughters scold their mothers.
"For their own good."

ODILE DORMEUIL

Mothers&Daughters

The love between mother and daughter,
webbed together like flesh and bones, Ma Ma,
a love which, I am learning now, passed between us too,
that always was between us, even if silent and hidden
in the deepest regions of ourselves…

SUSAN GRIFFIN, B. 1943

Mothers&Daughters

Like it or not, we are bound to one another.
It is the lightest of links – so light that sometimes
we seem to forget it altogether.
But it is stronger than life itself.

PAM BROWN 1928 – 2014

Mothers&Daughters

We've had some fights, you and I.
The sort that only we could have and still be friends.
(I like it most when we end up laughing!)

SIÂN E. MORGAN, B. 1973

Mothers&Daughters

My mother taught me to walk
proud and tall "as if the world was mine".

SOPHIA LOREN, B. 1934

Mothers&Daughters

The times we spent together
took on a special intimacy,
a quality that I remember best
from the day I woke up
and my daughter was brought to me
in hospital.
I won't top that feeling
in my lifetime.

TAMMY GRIMES

Mothers&Daughters

Your smiles are the currency of joy
and I am a millionaire of your happiness.

LINDA MACFARLANE, B. 1953

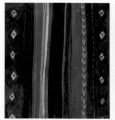   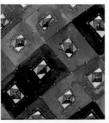

Mothers&Daughters

I can be bold and brave. Face down committees.
Climb a mountain. Deal with a storm at sea.
But sometimes when my courage wears a little thin
I yearn for a hug from you.
"Hold on, Love. You can do it."

CHARLOTTE GRAY

Mothers&Daughters

I started awake to hear distant yelling.
I didn't know her cry until I heard it
and then I knew that I could pick it out
from any other. A woman can live for
thirty-four-years and not know
she is equipped with sonar.
I tracked the baby down
like a need-seeking missile.

ALLISON PEARSON, B. 1960

Mothers&Daughters

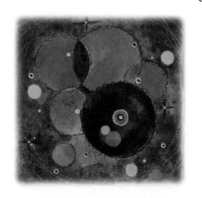

I know if I turned up on the doorstep in the middle of the night, soaked through, with all my bags and speechless with tears you'd just say; "Oh, Love. Take off all your clothes. Put on my big woolly dressing gown." Let's hope it will never come to that. But it's nice to know.

PAM BROWN 1928 – 2014

Mothers&Daughters

I used to jump you over puddles, lift you down from walls,
rescue you from quagmires, towel you dry.
And now you must lend me a hand on steps and stairs,
give me a leg up into taxis, dust me down when I have fallen flat.
We take good care of each other,
you and I.

PAMELA DUGDALE

Mothers&Daughters

I loved my baby,
I loved my budding ballet dancer,
I loved my argumentative adolescent.
But most of all I love the friend
that my daughter has become.

LINDA MACFARLANE, B. 1953

APRIL 20

Love me always and forever, my existence depends on it...
you are all my joy and my sorrow.
What remains of my life is overshadowed by grief when I consider
how much of it will be spent far from you.

MADAME DE SÉVIGNÉ 1626 – 1696

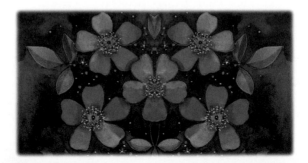

Mothers&Daughters

How could I explain the enormous
feeling of security in knowing
that now she was with me in the world?...
We would discuss everything in life...
and help each other be real people.

LIV ULLMANN, B. 1939

APRIL 19

The relationship between a mother
and a daughter is as varied,
as mysterious, as constantly changing
and interconnected as the patterns
that touch, move away from,
and touch again in a kaleidoscope.

LYN LIFSHIN

Mothers&Daughters

One day your daughter
will banish all the menfolk.
Announce that you have flu
and see you into bed.
And Take Over.

ODILE DORMEUIL

Mothers&Daughters

A mother is a person
who seeing there are only four pieces
of pie for five people,
promptly announces
she never did care for pie.

TENNEVA JORDAN

Mothers&Daughters

For my daughter and I, it is my dream
that an open, loving, sharing relationship
will always prevail over one with conflicts.
When my daughter looks in a mirror
in her adult life, I want her to see herself,
but know she has had a mother who has loved
and supported her.

CHERYL D. DEAN

Mothers & Daughters

Somehow, the battles are behind us. We shop together – taking delight in the sheer awfulness of much of the stuff displayed. Borrow each other's umbrellas. Are cheerfully rude to one another. Swap opinions. Even rant a little over the issues that disturbed our minds. Still mother and child. But friends to boot. Contemporaries.

ODILE DORMEUIL

SEPTEMBER 18

I wrapped you in protection, yet each time telling myself
"Teach her to clad herself in armor and be brave.
I must remember to love her enough to let her fall."

DONNA GREEN

Mothers & Daughters

People said – she's far too young
to sit through Bohème, to eat olives,
to crew a dinghy,
to stand in the snow and watch the stars fall.
You took no notice.
Thank you for being my trusting mother!

PAM BROWN 1928 – 2014

Mothers&Daughters

Mothers and daughters madden each other at times.
But they go on worrying about each other as long as they live.

PAM BROWN 1928 – 2014

Mothers&Daughters

Mother darling,
It is wonderful to meet and talk over everything
and share and laugh and understand each other's situations
as no one else can.

ANNE MORROW LINDBERGH 1906 – 2001

SEPTEMBER 20

I am loved.
I am valued.
That is the best start in life
for any daughter.

CHARLOTTE GRAY

Mothers&Daughters

...the daughter never ever gives up
on the mother,
just as the mother never gives up
on the daughter.
There is a tie here so strong
that nothing can break it.
I called it "the unbreakable bond".

RACHEL BILLINGTON, B. 1942

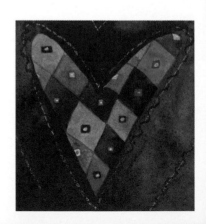

Mothers&Daughters

She gave us Spring, That we could watch crocus grow,
She gave us Summer, That we could splash in the sea,
She gave us Autumn, She gave us Winter,
That we could fill the house with toys.
All this and more... Filling our years with seasons,
Filling our lives with joy.

LINDA MACFARLANE, B. 1953

Mothers&Daughters

When all my troubles seem unbearable, I seek you out.
I know that you can't solve them but I tell you
my problems anyway. You always listen, not judging, not trying
to provide a quick fix solution. And when I'm finished talking
the problems don't seem half as bad.

LINDA MACFARLANE, B. 1953

Mothers&Daughters

I f your daughter is different but right
stand by her, shoulder to shoulder.

PAMELA DUGDALE

APRIL 12

Slowly, slowly, slowly the roles are reversed
and the daughter becomes the one who nags a little,
cares a lot and worries all the time.

PAMELA DUGDALE

Thank you!
Thank you for thinking up the little
things you do, and then doing them.

AUTHOR UNKNOWN

Mothers&Daughters

I love your smiles,
I see them everywhere.
No matter where I am.
No matter where you are,
your smiles
will always stay with me.

SIÂN E. MORGAN, B. 1973

Mothers&Daughters

She is yours to hold in your cupped hands,
to guard and to guide. Give her your strength and wisdom
and all the good that life can offer. Yours is a sacred trust.
Never harm her with words that can bite and sting.

MICHELE GUINNESS

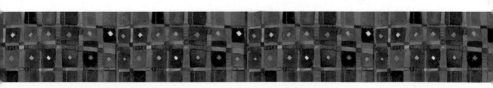

APRIL 10

What feeling is so nice as a child's hand in yours?
So small, so soft and warm, like a kitten huddling
in the shelter of your clasp.

MARJORIE HOLMES 1910 – 2002

Mothers&Daughters

Sensible mothers let their children sleep. Mothers like you take them out of bed to see a shower of falling stars.

PAM BROWN 1928 – 2014

Mothers&Daughters

...I encouraged you to claim your life
and fight like hell for your right to be;
and the best gift that I could ever give to you
was to say "yes" to your dreams
that were not my own.

MARGARET SLOAN-HUNTER 1947 – 2004

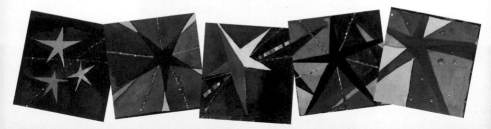

SEPTEMBER 26

I have learned to really hear the message
my mother has given me all my life:
"I will be with you always." As in forever,
into the eternal hereafter, no matter what.

REBECCA WALKER

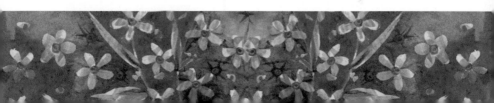

Mothers & Daughters

Thank you, for getting me out of bed
to see a shower of falling stars.
Thank you for taking me on bus rides
to the end of the line.
Thank you for making a walk
an excitement.
Thank you for treats when times
were hard.
Thank you for being there.
Always and always.

PAM BROWN 1928 – 2014

Mothers&Daughters

A daughter's hug is the greatest wealth a parent can know.

STUART & LINDA MACFARLANE

Mothers&Daughters

Thank you for your sayings which turned out
to be vital.

– Always say thank you.

– Wash your neck.

– Spit out bones, fruit stones, scalding potatoes
whatever the company.

– Go to the loo whenever the opportunity offers.

– Never be panicked by knives
and forks or wine waiters.

ODILE DORMEUIL

Mothers&Daughters

No mother and daughter
ever live apart,
no matter what the distance
between them.

CHRISTIE WATSON

Mothers&Daughters

She broke the bread into two fragments and gave them
to her children, who ate them with eagerness.
"She hath saved none for herself," grumbled the Sergeant.
"Because she is not hungry," said the soldier.
"No," said the Sergeant.
"Because she is a mother."

VICTOR HUGO 1802 – 1885

Mothers&Daughters

My dream for Ashley and Alexandra
is to raise them to be
all they can be...
human beings who not only find,
but aren't afraid to go after,
whatever it is that makes them
happy in life.

VANESSA BELL CALLOWAY

Mothers&Daughters

Know that I am your greatest ally and fan.
I will continue to applaud at your victories and walk with you
through trials and mistakes.
I look in your face and am proud of who we are –
and even more, proud of who I am because of the honor
and privilege of being your mother.

MOLLY

Mothers&Daughters

*I know you're always
there for me
But never forget
I'm here for you.*

PAM BROWN 1928 – 2014

APRIL 4

You taught me that it's possible to love someone
so much that it actually hurts.

LINDA MACFARLANE, B. 1953

Mothers&Daughters

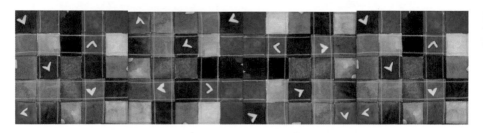

Call your mother. Tell her you love her.
Remember, you're the only person who knows
what her heart sounds like from inside.

RACHEL WOLCHIN

Mothers&Daughters

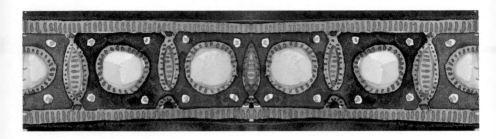

If an experience in childhood still brings an agony
of embarrassment – one's mother is guaranteed to relate it
at a dinner for the in-laws.

PAMELA DUGDALE

Mothers&Daughters

An elderly mother contemplates her elderly daughter
and is amazed. So short a time ago she was clutching at her skirt.
So short a time ago she was clinging to her hand. And here she is,
capable, experienced, with children of her own and, more astounding
still, a grandma. And yet, and yet her own dear daughter.
Her child forever.

PAMELA DUGDALE

APRIL 2

For the twenty-two thousand
or so smiles.
For your belief in me,
for forgivings and kind words,
thank you.

HELEN M. EXLEY

Mothers&Daughters

In passing we may say that a girl is always safe
who gives a wise and loving mother her entire confidence,
and a mother is her child's very best counsellor and chaperone.

MARGARET E. SANGSTER 1838 – 1912

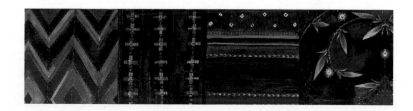

Mothers&Daughters

I miss our nature walks in the early spring, discovering the first forsythia and a host of daffodils smiling brightly in the warm, fragrant spring air… I miss the beach days, the swim meets, the ribbons.

ALEXANDRA STODDARD

OCTOBER 4

A birthday card that's an explosion of crayon
with "To Mum" scrolled across the front,
a drawing of a pink three legged rabbit,
lovingly hand sewn. These are a daughter's gifts
of love; a mother's treasury.

LISETTE FAVIER

MARCH 31

Mother's voice clings
to my heart
like trails of bedstraw
that catch you in the lanes.

MARY WEBB 1881 – 1927

Mothers&Daughters

In an uncertain world you are my certainty.

PAM BROWN 1928 – 2014

MARCH 30

A mother is someone you phone out of duty
then talk to for hours out of love.

LISETTE FAVIER

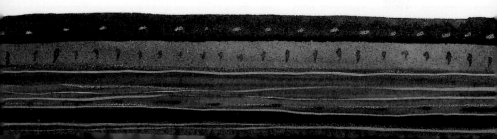

Mothers&Daughters

Thank you
for the precious years,
for times
I will remember
my whole life.

HELEN M. EXLEY

MARCH 29

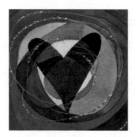

Still, even though I travel to the very edges of the earth,
I turn to you, as if you were by my side, and share the moment.
"Look, Mum, look!"
As when you showed me the world.

PAM BROWN 1928 – 2014

Mothers&Daughters

OCTOBER 7

You nurse me when I'm feeling ill. You pamper me even when I'm well. You don't just go the extra mile – you do the whole marathon.

LINDA MACFARLANE, B. 1953

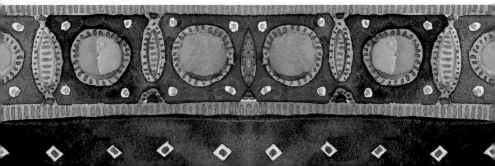

MARCH   28

...when they put your first child into your arms,
perhaps you will think of me –
that it was a high moment in my life
too when for the first time I held you,
a little red bundle, in my arms.

ROSE SCHOSINGER 1907 – 1943

Mothers&Daughters

And when I look at her beautiful slender body moving here
and moving there in eager anticipation of womanhood – her eyes,
one moment sparkling, the next full of impatient tears,
her sudden hugs and confessions, and her wonderful new spirit –
I realize that she evokes homesickness in me.
Homesick for the days when everything was possible.

LIV ULLMANN, B. 1939

Mothers&Daughters

*Nothing can mend a heavy heart
like a daughter's laughter.*

LINDA MACFARLANE, B. 1953

OCTOBER 9

Everyone else gives me the expected for gifts.
YOU give me astonishments.

PAMELA DUGDALE

Mothers&Daughters

We have filled the house with a lifetime of laughter
crammed with so many happy memories.

SIÂN E. MORGAN, B. 1973

Mothers&Daughters

She is very touching in her
sweet little marks of affection.
Once or twice,
when I have seemed unhappy
about little things,
she has come and held up her
sweet mouth to be kissed.

MRS ELIZABETH GASKELL
1810 – 1865

Mothers&Daughters

On this doorstep I stand
year after year
and watch you leaving
and think: May you not
skin your knees. May you
not catch your fingers
in car doors. May
our hearts not break...

EVANGELINE PATERSON

OCTOBER 11

A Child of Happiness
always seems like an old soul living in a new body,
and her face is very serious until she smiles,
and then the sun lights up the world…

ANNE CAMERON, B. 1938

Mothers&Daughters

Even now, I can still feel my hand safe in your hand, the softness of your cheek,the hug that headed off sorrow, the kiss that healed all pain. Held in memory so vivid that they have never faded. You have taught me how to love.

PAM BROWN 1928 – 2014

Mothers&Daughters

Mothers are not put on this Earth
to be equal. They are there to offer services
from taxi driver to banker, bedroom tidier
to chef and to offer unconditional,
unquestioning and endless love in good times
and bad with thanks or no thanks.

CHRISTA ACKROYD, B. 1957

Mothers&Daughters

My mum is a nurse when we are ill, a gardener,
a chef, cooks super meals, a waitress, a decorator, a chamber-maid,
a dressmaker when she makes or knits our clothes,
a fruit-picker, a book-keeper…

JULIE, AGE 13

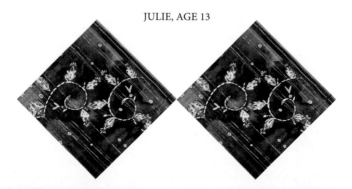

Mothers&Daughters

So often you put your hand in mine
or we link arms and step out in the world together,
just spellbound in amazement.

SIÂN E. MORGAN, B. 1973

Mothers&Daughters

I hope you find joy in the great things of life –
but also in the little things.
A flower, a song, a butterfly on your hand.

ELLEN LEVINE

Mothers & Daughters

It's good when a mother and her daughter...
store things in their minds to tell each other.
People they've met, things they've done, delights....
Small threads that bind them together in love
and understanding.

PAM BROWN 1928 – 2014

MARCH 21

Total, unconditional, unending –
the love a mother feels for a daughter.

MATHILDE FORESTIER

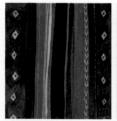   

Mothers & Daughters

*A mother's daughter
is never a failure
in anything she does.*

STUART & LINDA MACFARLANE

MARCH 20

Dear You. Dear Friend. Always.

PAMELA DUGDALE

Mothers&Daughters

I had a little girl.
So small. So utterly dependent.
Held in my arms.
But so inquisitive. So daring.
Getting ready to take on the world.
And here she is,
grown and independent
and, somehow, it seems in no time at all,
heading a family!
I stretch my arms a little further
to embrace them all!

CHARLOTTE GRAY

Mothers&Daughters

Thank you, Mom, for all the dirty dishes you've washed,
the wet laundry you've hung out to dry. Thank you for the countless
ways you've given your love, your wisdom, your strength
and your words of encouragement.
Most of all, thanks for always being there when I needed you.

COOKIE CURCI

Mothers&Daughters

 A daughter in the depths of despair
will still cry for her mother — even if she's half a world away.

HANNAH KLEIN

Mothers&Daughters

Mother, throughout the years we have shared so much;
we have shared good times, we have shared bad times,
we have even, on occasion, shared our clothes.
But the chocolate cake in the fridge! Forget it – it's mine, all mine!

LINDA MACFARLANE, B. 1953

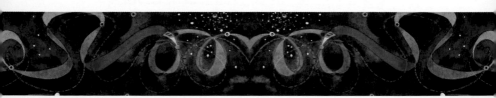

Mothers&Daughters

When I stopped seeing
my mother with the eyes
of a child, I saw a woman
who helped me give birth
to myself.

NANCY FRIDAY, B. 1933

MARCH 17

Thank you for remembering
my stories, loving my made-up games
in the backyard
and saying all your friends
loved the birthday parties
I over-organised!

LYNN MCLEAN

Mothers & Daughters

When a woman has a baby it is her mother,
not her father, she turns to, and if that baby is a girl,
in due time, she will turn to her mother.
That is a real family tree. The family tree of women.

RACHEL BILLINGTON, B. 1942

Mothers&Daughters

You are like an everlasting friendship.
You are like the beginning, end and everything in between.
You are like a very knowledgeable volume of encyclopaedias.
You are like you and I love you.

LAUREL O. HOYE, AGE 8

OCTOBER 20

Out of your life
you wove my life.
But that was not enough.
You gave me love.
Protection. Patience. Kindness.
Guidance and forgiveness.
You taught me how to live.

ODILE DORMEUIL

Mothers&Daughters

MARCH 15

Little Girl
My Stringbean,
My Lovely Woman.

ANNE SEXTON 1928 – 1974

Mothers & Daughters

Time and distance mean very little
to mothers and daughters who love each other.
They can always find a way
to reach out to each other,
Comfort each other, give each other courage.

CHARLOTTE GRAY

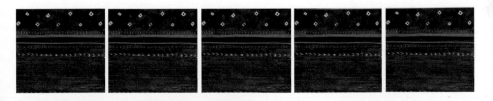

Mothers&Daughters

I didn't need to seek out love,
I got more than my share of that from my daughter.
She and I were a solid unit,
and I had a lot to learn from her…

MARSHA HUNT, B. 1946

Mothers&Daughters

When I was hurt,
when I was afraid,
you were always there,
giving me comfort
and encouragement.
Then and now.

PAM BROWN 1928 – 2014

Mothers&Daughters

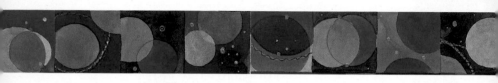

What's a shopping expedition
without you to share it?
To giggle over the ridiculous,
to exclaim at the magnificent,
to hold each other back
– or egg each other on.

PAM BROWN 1928 – 2014

OCTOBER 23

You have grown into a kind person - that's the best.
You are a lovely, achieving, strong young woman.
I can't be proud of you, because you have achieved it
all by yourself. But I can say thank you — just for being
my awesome daughter.

CHRISTINE BANNING

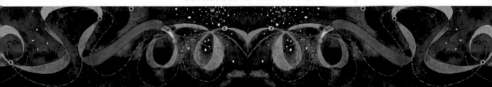

Mothers&Daughters

...We have written to each other
of our plans, problems, hopes,
achievements, disappointments
and successes, as well as our day to day
happenings. Our letters have been
a strong life-line stretched
half way around the world:
to me they are a continuous message
of love and dependence...

IVY SPENDER

Mothers & Daughters

Whether it was a failed exam,
a missing passport, or a broken leg,
you always remained calm and said to me,
"Don't worry – everything will be all right".
And somehow, you made it so.

LINDA MACFARLANE, B. 1953

Mothers&Daughters

The pain of missing her daughter
is more than compensated for when a mother sees
the strong, independent woman her baby has become.

MATHILDE FORESTIER

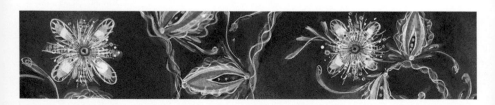

Mothers&Daughters

Anything is better when we share it.

PAMELA DUGDALE

Mothers&Daughters

My life bridges the past and the future with both
my mother and my daughter. To experience
one who baked all her own bread, or felt unworthy,
and see another vie for president and CEO of
a Fortune 500 company and feel unworthy,
is an astonishing experience that I could never
have without both being and having
a wonderful mother and daughter.

LYNN WILSON SPOHRER

Mothers&Daughters

...you must always think well of yourself and realize
your own worth. You are a pearl of great value.
Don't ever forget those things, especially in your darkest
moments. During my darkest moments I wasn't able to do
a lot for you, but I hope you always knew I loved you.
I know you love me.

TEENA

Mothers&Daughters

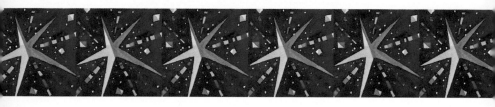

You clasped your tiny hand in mine and I knew,
no matter what life would bring, we would never let go.

LINDA MACFARLANE, B. 1953

Mothers&Daughters

Thank you
for all the small
surprises,
the hugs,
the smiles,
the secrets.

PAM BROWN 1928 – 2014

Mothers&Daughters

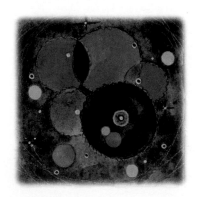

All good mums
can send love down
the telephone.
Or in a brown paper parcel.
Or an envelope.
Tucked into a suitcase.
Hidden in a haversack.

PAMELA DUGDALE

Mothers&Daughters

A daughter knows her mother's special favourite flower, her special music, her Top Treat... — And acts upon it.

HANNAH KLEIN

Mothers&Daughters

My mommy is very nice inside her and very nice outside.
Very nice inside means she is not spiteful...
She is very kind, and very nice on the outsides means
she looked beautiful.

SIOBHAN, AGE 7

Mothers & Daughters

She phones me regularly
to keep tabs on me.
When I'm not tranquil,
she will try to steady me.
My periods of loneliness,
she reassures me.
What a marvellous daughter she is!

ROMILDA VILLANI

Mothers&Daughters

No one else could be so easily forgiven
for dropping everything across chairs, beds and floors.
No one but you.
Even if we don't always see eye to eye,
it always works out in the end.
I could never stay cross with you for long.

SIÂN E. MORGAN, B. 1973

OCTOBER 30

Always and now in my eyes, heart, and soul,
you are to me the most beautiful bud, the loveliest bloom,
and the most perfect flower. I've loved you
from the day you were born. I love you with every
breath you take. I will love you forever.
Love Mum

AUTHOR UNKNOWN

MARCH 5

...you catch yourself in a gesture, a look,
an expression that makes you think –
"that's just like Ma".
But it is also reassuring, for in the world
of a million changes, it reaffirms
the continuity of life, its eternal transmission
and mystery.

MARY KENNY, B. 1944

Mothers&Daughters

Observe any High Street or shopping mall on a Saturday and you'll see them – mothers and daughters, arm-in-arm, chatting, giggling, carrying bags, rushing home to look at what they've bought and have a good talk over a cup of tea. When it works, the bond between the two females is a unique link.

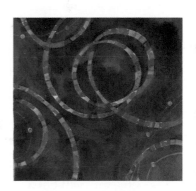

BEL MOONEY, B. 1946

Mothers & Daughters

My mother and I walk through the rooms of her house…
Our white muslin skirts billow up around our ankles,
our hair hangs straight down our backs as our arms
hang straight at our sides…
As we walk through the rooms, we merge and separate,
merge and separate; soon
we shall enter the final stage of our evolution.

JAMAICA KINCAID, B. 1949

Mothers&Daughters

My mum is a never ending song in my heart of comfort,
happiness, and being. I may sometimes forget
the words but I always remember the tune.

GRAYCIE HARMON

Mothers&Daughters

Motherhood changed me because it is so fundamental
what you're doing for another person.
And you are able to do it even though it takes a lot.

MEG RYAN

NOVEMBER 2

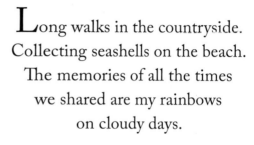

Long walks in the countryside.
Collecting seashells on the beach.
The memories of all the times
we shared are my rainbows
on cloudy days.

LINDA MACFARLANE, B. 1953

Mothers&Daughters

In one's teens, one inevitably considers one's mother
to be nagging, narrow-minded, distrustful and evil-tempered.
Until, decades later, one is lying awake in the dark,
listening for the sound of car engines
and rehearsing the policeman's knock.

ODILE DORMEUIL

NOVEMBER 3

Children go through a time
when they like to
shock their elders.
Parents look back at their
own youth –
and try to oblige.

PAMELA DUGDALE

MARCH 1

Frazzled nerves, sleepless nights, spoiled dinners, blocked drains, trodden flower beds… Thank you for forgiving me.

PAM BROWN 1928 – 2014

Mothers&Daughters

She is so very new, so very small.
But time is ticking. She has everything to learn,
ten thousand discoveries to make.
– Find delight in her astonishment. In every skill
she finds. Rediscover wonder. Too soon she'll smile
and turn away and set out on her own adventures.
Leaving you her childhood to remember.
But part of you forever.

ODILE DORMEUIL

Mothers & Daughters

A mother is someone
who sings in the kitchen.

ELISABETH FENTON

You make the house
a happy place to be.

SIAN FITZPATRICK, AGE 8

NOVEMBER 5

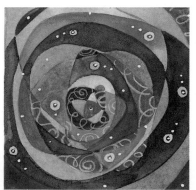

And I love all those sentences
that start with "I need your help."
I can be useful or
I can simply be there,
holding my breath,
watching and waiting as you
make decisions for yourself.

SIÂN E. MORGAN, B. 1973

Mothers&Daughters

Mother and daughter share a unique bond of love.
A bond that gives each strength and courage.
A bond that enriches each life.
A bond that makes every achievement more pleasing
and every hardship more bearable.
An unbreakable bond that grows with each passing year.

STUART & LINDA MACFARLANE

Mothers&Daughters

You've given me more love and joy than most mothers and daughters ever share. I'd do it all again just for the honour and the wonder of being your mother.

AUTHOR UNKNOWN

Mothers&Daughters

We talked together of books that have been important.
We shared the overwhelming delight in a picture,
a play, a poem, a piece of music. We cheered for the same team.
We loved walking the high hills.
These things are what made me what I am.

AUTHOR UNKNOWN

A daughter may outgrow your lap, but she will never outgrow your love.

AUTHOR UNKNOWN

Mothers&Daughters

When you are a mother,
you are never really alone
in your thoughts.
You are connected to your child
and to all those
who touch your lives.

SOPHIA LOREN, B. 1934

Mothers & Daughters

Thank you, for finding house room
for pebbles and great chunks of rock,
for twigs and branches
and small saplings, for wriggly things
in jars, for collections of china pigs,
posters of pop idols.

PAM BROWN 1928 – 2014

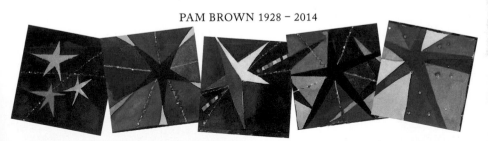

Mothers&Daughters

Growing up is tricky.
There's so much to learn,
so many things to try.
Mistakes to make.
But you have been there,
patient and forgiving
kind and understanding.
Strong.
A certainty when everything
seemed confusion.
A safe haven.

PAMELA DUGDALE

Mothers&Daughters

Sometimes the greatest comfort
is to return to the nest and be a little child again.
Hot water bottles, tea and sympathy.

CHARLOTTE GRAY

Mothers&Daughters

A loving and careful mother both recognises
and even protects her daughter's autonomy
and also helps her dance out confidently on to a wider stage.

RACHEL BILLINGTON, B. 1942

Mothers&Daughters

You taught me how to talk and walk and read.
But more importantly you taught me how to care and love.

LINDA MACFARLANE, B. 1953

FEBRUARY 22

I've got a beautiful wooden box
for my necklaces and rings,
but my real treasures are inside
an old baby milk tin.
There you'll find
your hospital baby bracelet,
your first shoe, a lock of hair...
your first drawing,
your first story...

LINDA MACFARLANE, B. 1953

Mothers&Daughters

Coming home seemed to have started the healing process.
No longer vivid and garish, the memories seemed to be covered
in gossamer, fading behind a curtain of time and forgiveness.

KAREN FOWLER

Mothers&Daughters

She doesn't tell you
everything.
She loves you far too much.

ODILE DORMEUIL

Mothers&Daughters

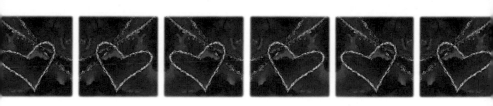

We have to let go their hands.
But the joys we knew before, remembered or lost,
are part of us all forever.

PAMELA DUGDALE

Mothers & Daughters

From the very moment I was born,
you insisted that I was myself
and not an extension of you and Dad –
that I had not come into existence
simply for you to organize
or even to love.
Thank you for giving me
the freedom to love you.

PAM BROWN 1928 – 2014

Mothers & Daughters

A mother's love for her child
is like nothing else in the world.
It knows no law, no pity.
It dares all things and crushes down remorselessly
all that stands in its path.

AGATHA CHRISTIE 1890 – 1976

Mothers&Daughters

In the sheltered simplicity of the first days after a baby is born,
one sees again the magical closed circle, the miraculous
sense of two people existing only for each other, the tranquil sky
reflected on the face of the mother nursing her child.

ANNE MORROW LINDBERGH 1906 – 2001

NOVEMBER 14

You painted my childhood a magical kaleidoscope.

LINDA MACFARLANE, B. 1953

Mothers&Daughters

And so our mothers and grandmothers have,
more often than not anonymously,
handed on the creative spark,
the seed of the flower they themselves never hoped to see,
or like a sealed letter they could not plainly read.

ALICE WALKER, B. 1944

Mothers&Daughters

It's my experience that women look to their mothers
at the time when they are having their own children.
It is a visceral tie. Talking of how they themselves
came into the world with the very woman who was involved
is reassuring, a source of traditional advice and as emotionally
bonding as any human relationship can be.

JOAN BAKEWELL, B. 1933

Mothers&Daughters

We ring each other to say,
"Goodnight, God bless."
and, "Good Morning."
If she rings me first,
I know it's to see if I'm still alive.
We never stop laughing and we never
stop crying when we are together.

DAME THORA HIRD 1911 – 2003

Mothers&Daughters

...As she grew older she began to favour me, and nothing gave me
more delight than her evident preference...
I certainly had not anticipated such wreathing, dazzling gaiety
of affection from her whenever I happened to catch her eye.

MARGARET DRABBLE, B. 1939

Mothers&Daughters

FEBRUARY 16

Writing this has just made me fill up with love for you.
It is such a privilege to grow with you, Jodie.
I will try to encourage you to face up to hard things,
and please will you encourage me to do the same?

SUSAN

Mothers&Daughters

The world spins. Times change. And yet –
a mother is as much a mother as she was five thousand years ago.
And daughters as loving and demanding
– and always astonishing.

PAM BROWN 1928 – 2014

Mothers&Daughters

Mothers
and daughters
delight in each other's
adventures.

PAMELA DUGDALE

Mothers&Daughters

A daughter is a mother's gender partner, her closest ally in the family confederacy, an extension of her self. And mothers are their daughters' role model, their biological and emotional road map, the arbiter of all their relationships.

VICTORIA SECUNDA

Mothers&Daughters

Whenever I had a broken heart,
you healed that with kindness.
Whenever my dreams didn't come true,
you replaced the void with kindness.
Thank goodness,
your kindness never seems to run out.

SIÂN E. MORGAN, B. 1973

Mothers&Daughters

Mothers and daughters
have an indefinable bond,
Unspoken, undeniable, unending.
I feel your pain,
I celebrate your joy,
I share your dreams,
...because you are my daughter
and I am your mother.

LINDA MACFARLANE, B. 1953

Mothers&Daughters

She was my firstborn.
No child was ever more wanted, more adored.
I had a very special delight in her,
cuddly closeness with her,
and understanding with her.

PATRICIA NEAL 1926 – 2010

Mothers&Daughters

I could sit down and list
all that you've done for me.
But I'd run out of paper
and ten pens would run dry.

CHARLOTTE GRAY

Mothers&Daughters

A mother looks into the eyes
of her baby daughter and sends her love,
joy, hope and peace.
A mother looks into the eyes of her
grown up daughter and sends her love,
joy, hope and peace.
Because being a mother never stops.

MATHILDE FORESTIER

Mothers&Daughters

The truth is, the most effective way to inculcate in our daughters
a fighting chance at life-long self-love and empowerment is not
in the books we read to them, or the workshops we send them to,
or the media we do or do not expose them to, or even the things
we tell them, rather it is in the reflection of self-love
and empowerment they see in us, their mothers.

MELIA KEETON-DIGBY

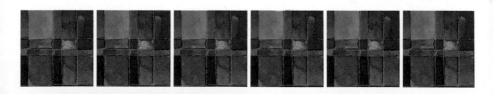

Mothers&Daughters

You're more confident than me,
You're smarter than me,
You're kinder than me.
Wow! I did a great job!

LINDA MACFARLANE, B. 1953

Mothers&Daughters

Everyone needs
a mother.
And some who are
very lucky,
like me,
have an awesome one
like you.

PAMELA DUGDALE

Thank you, my dearest girl, for telling me when your friend
is in trouble, even though there's nothing I can do to be of any help.
Thank you for the phone call to tell me of a TV documentary
that's just starting. Thank you for asking me for recipes.
Thank you for giving me advice.
Thank you for letting me into your life.

PAM BROWN 1928 – 2014

Mothers&Daughters

If I was a queen
I would give you anything in the world –
like me being a good girl.

HAYLY BENNETT

FEBRUARY 9

As for my girls, I'll raise them to think they breathe fire.

JESSICA KIRKLAND

Mothers&Daughters

If there is anything in my life
that can be of value to you,
I want you to have it;
if I can save you a stumble or a
single false step, I want to do it.

FLORENCE WENDEROTH SAUNDERS, D. 1926

Mothers&Daughters

Mothers give unconditionally.
They give a lifetime.
And "thank you"
will never be enough.

HELEN M. EXLEY

Mothers&Daughters

Even if I've been to a place a hundred times before,
it feels different when I go there with you.
Almost like I've never been before, almost like I see it
through your eyes, with more excitement,
anticipation than before.

SIÂN E. MORGAN, B. 1973

Mothers&Daughters

...at the end of the day
she's the most important thing.
Just being daft together –
that's what I enjoy most
about being with my daughter.

LORRAINE KELLY, B. 1959

Mothers&Daughters

Probably there is nothing in human nature more resonant with charges than the flow of energy between two biologically alike bodies, one of which has lain in amniotic bliss inside the other, one of which has labored to give birth to the other.

ADRIENNE RICH 1929 – 2012

Mothers&Daughters

Daughters in your attic
will come across boxes,
lift the lid and find
every letter that they ever wrote,
and cards, and finger paintings.
Lopsided little pots and lino cuts.
Photographs and ticket stubs.
Their lives preserved in amber.

PAMELA DUGDALE

Mothers&Daughters

Thank you for making me feel
that nothing that you have achieved
is worth more than my love.

PAM BROWN 1928 – 2014

Mothers&Daughters

Our first mother-daughter outing:
For three hours, knitting our thoughts and lives together
like old college roommates going toward a reunion.

PHYLLIS THEROUX, B. 1939

Mothers&Daughters

A daughter is a blessing of a very special kind.
She'll "borrow" your best perfume.
She'll never tidy her room.
She'll make the bathroom her second home.
She'll fill your life and heart with a love
greater than words can express.

LINDA MACFARLANE, B. 1953

Mothers&Daughters

I even love her bones.
We are so close.
She is my very best friend.

FAITH BROWN, B. 1944

Mothers&Daughters

...when my daughter walks back into my world, the sun shines
and my heart fills once more with love and light,
giving me a whole new reason to feel joy.

GOLDIE HAWN, B. 1945

Mothers&Daughters

Daughters rather enjoy one's getting old.
For now it is their turn to nag a little,
and scold, and be exasperated.

ODILE DORMEUIL

Mothers&Daughters

The joys of being a mother are as special
as being a daughter. On that alone we are equal.

CHRISTA ACKROYD, B. 1957

Mothers&Daughters

You care…
That I am happy.
That I am healthy.
That I enjoy my job.
That I have good friends.
That I find true love.
More than anyone in the world, a mother cares.

LINDA MACFARLANE, B. 1953

Mothers&Daughters

DECEMBER 1

...two people as deeply bound to each other
as a mother and her daughter are never really separated,
even by death.

RITA RUDNER, B. 1953

Mothers&Daughters

*Whatever comes our love for each other is constant.
Our sure anchor in any storm.*

PAM BROWN 1928 – 2014

An image comes to me. I see generations of women
bearing flame. It is hidden, buried deep within,
yet they are handing it down from one to another,
burning. And now, in this very moment,
my mother imparts the care of it to me.
I must hand it on when the time comes to my daughter.

KIM CHERNIN, B. 1940

Mothers&Daughters

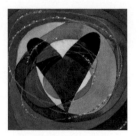

She holds out her hand to air,
Sea, sky, wind, sun, movement, stillness.
And wants to hold them all.
My finger is her earth connection, me, and earth.

JENNIFER ARMITAGE

Mothers&Daughters

There is something infinitely precious about having a daughter. Mine, my daughter, from the moment she was born, drew from me reserves of tenderness, protectiveness and fight I never knew I possessed.

MICHELE GUINNESS

Mothers&Daughters

I think life began
with waking up
and loving
my mother's face.

GEORGE ELIOT (MARY ANN EVANS)
1819 – 1880

Mothers&Daughters

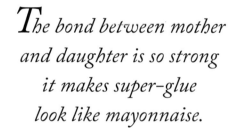

*The bond between mother
and daughter is so strong
it makes super-glue
look like mayonnaise.*

STUART & LINDA MACFARLANE

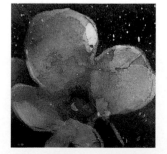

Mothers&Daughters

My mother... she is roses and London gardens,
she is wartime movies and Frank Sinatra songs, she is
Italy and France, and China tea. She is soaked through
everything I see. I look at my face in the mirror, at my mannerisms,
the veins in my hands and realise she will always be with me.

HARRIET WALTER, B. 1950

Mothers&Daughters

Thank you for the train rides
and the roller coasters.
Thank you for running with me
in the rain.
And sprawling with me
in the summer sun.

PAM BROWN 1928 – 2014

Mothers&Daughters

I rebelled.
Brought you to tears sometimes,
trying on different selves,
as the young must do.
And always you were patient.
Buoyed up by love and hope and trust
– and here we are.
Friends. Companions.
Mother and loving daughter.

PAMELA DUGDALE

Mothers&Daughters

Hurrah for technology! A thousand miles between us
and yet you are here, nose to nose, the dear girl
I have always known. Close as ever. Never lost.
My friend, my daughter.

CHARLOTTE GRAY

Mothers&Daughters

May you be blessed with faith, courage,
patience and love throughout your life experience.
I will always be there for you.

TEENA

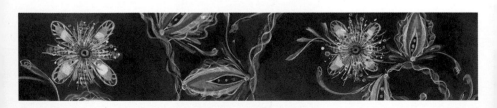

Mothers&Daughters

And yet, Ma Ma, this is what makes me cry now,
not all those injuries but the simple syllables of a love,
buried for years, which is being revealed to me even
at this moment. It is that love a child bears a mother,
hot and steamy as food, implacable as night, irrefutable
as dreams insinuating their strange reason into daylight.

SUSAN GRIFFIN, B. 1943

Mothers&Daughters

Daughters never stop learning from their mothers
and mothers never stop marvelling at their daughters.

STUART & LINDA MACFARLANE

DECEMBER 8

The first time
I set eyes on you
I learned the meaning
of unconditional love.

MATHILDE FORESTIER

Mothers&Daughters

"Don't negotiate with terrorists,"
cautions her father when she yodels to be picked up.
Absolutely right of course.
But when he's left the room, I find myself
moving towards her, drawn by that irresistible beat.

ALLISON PEARSON, B. 1960

DECEMBER 9

Everybody needs someone to believe in them
– and for me that was YOU.

PAMELA DUGDALE

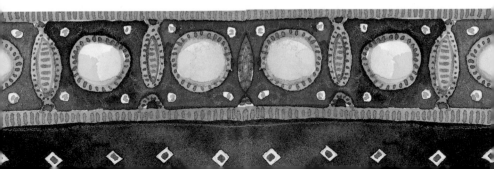

Mothers&Daughters

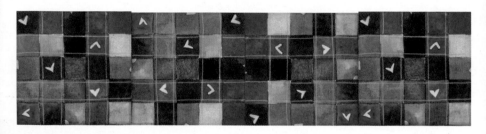

For cups of tea when I'm feeling poorly.
For offering advice when I'm feeling uncertain.
Thank you.

MATHILDE FORESTIER

Mothers&Daughters

My mother raised me, and then freed me.

MAYA ANGELOU 1928 – 2014

Mothers&Daughters

And as I grew, she shared good times with me.
She taught me to be realistic and understanding,
she taught me how a mother should be,
but most importantly, she taught me how to be a woman.

DEBRA DUEL, AGE 15

Mothers&Daughters

From the instant I saw her, a tiny red creature bathed
in the weird underwater light of the hospital operating room,
I loved her with an intensity that life
had not prepared me for.

SUSAN CHEEVER

Mothers&Daughters

Jenna, nearly sixteen years ago you entered this world as the first human being I had ever seen that shared my blood. I looked into your eyes when the nurse handed you to me and asked in amazement, "Where have I seen those eyes?" For the first time in my life, I felt a soul connection to another person.

KATHRYN

Mothers&Daughters

She is inventive, original
and takes what she wants from life –
including many of her mother's clothes!

RACHEL BILLINGTON, B. 1942

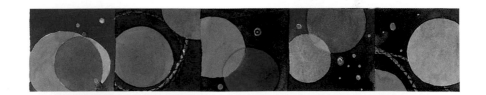

Mothers&Daughters

... a mother can be all-powerful, and she is the one
person who can make her family flourish.
All her juices are flowing; she feels alive –
she feels the vitality in her and in her girl child.
She is present and relevant and omniscient.
Such is the bond between a mother and daughter.

GOLDIE HAWN, B. 1945

Mothers&Daughters

Let me thank you for all the times
that I forgot to thank you – taking your love,
your patience and forgiveness for granted.

PAM BROWN 1928 – 2014

Mothers&Daughters

We played, we sang, we danced wildly. And we wandered quietly by the sea. I will always remember these days in summer – they're in my very being.

HELEN M. EXLEY

Mothers&Daughters

The love between a parent and child
is such a mystery. It is a unique love,
a love of unbound strength.
A love so precious that a mother
or father would give up their own life
to protect their child from harm.

STUART & LINDA MACFARLANE

JANUARY 19

The girl who changed the world.
She smiled and gave the flowers their colour,
She laughed and birds found they could sing,
She cried and the skies filled with rainbows,
She is the girl who changed the world,
She is life's miracle.

LINDA MACFARLANE, B. 1953

Mothers&Daughters

A true thank you for what you have done for me
would take a lifetime of service to back it.

HELEN THOMSON

Mothers&Daughters

I had discovered true love.
The love which repays slavery and exhaustion with a brief smile.
But what a smile!

SUE LIMB, B. 1946

DECEMBER 16

Dear Mummy

Thank you very much for the kind presents
that you give me and I like them very much.
and I like my guinea pig and it makes me
go to sleep. and I like you very much
and I hope you love me as well.
and you are very kind to me
when I am poorly and you make me happy.
Love Sally

SALLY ANDERSON, AGE 6

Mothers&Daughters

Whatever troubles
come between a mother
and her children – they are
one in blood and bone
and mind and heart.

PAM BROWN
1928 – 2014

Mothers&Daughters

W hat I wanted most for my daughter
was that she be able to soar confidently in her own sky,
wherever that might be…

HELEN CLAES

Mothers&Daughters

One day perhaps
you'll hold a child on your knee
and tell it the story I am telling now.
The one my mother told to me.
And back and back through history.

ODILE DORMEUIL

Mothers&Daughters

...you can do anything
you put your mind to...
Mom will give you
all the support, love, advice,
and help
you need to reach your goal.

SABRINA

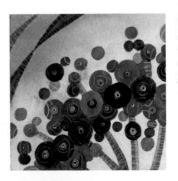

Mothers&Daughters

...my happiness is my daughter,
who is pretty and smart and laughing –
and who is my friend.

JOAN RIVERS 1933 – 2014

Mothers&Daughters

When I first laid eyes on Elizabeth and she on me,
it was recognition. I knew her, I knew that was what she looked like,
smelled like, sounded like. It was amazing because I could see
in her eyes that she knew me too, and was happy to finally
"eyeball" me, to touch me. I definitely felt a wave of love
flow back and forth.

PATRICIA BARTLETT

Mothers & Daughters

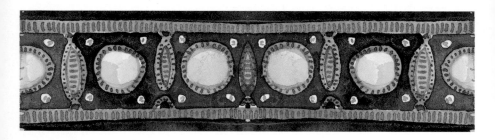

We are friends. We have loads of fun together, and our grooves
continue to sew the years into a beautiful tapestry.

ALEXANDRA STODDARD

DECEMBER 20

Thank you for making me feel wanted,
precious, irreplaceable.

PAM BROWN 1928 – 2014

Mothers&Daughters

Your pleasure in the simple acts of daily living taught me joy. Whenever I touch things that were yours or do something you did, unexpectedly you are with me, and I feel that joy.

TESS ENROTH 1925 – 2014

Her love is sustained and deep. Sometimes I feel like a drowning person, saved by the pulling and tugging, saved by the breath of air that is her caring.

BELL HOOKS, B. 1952

Mothers&Daughters

JANUARY 12

...she is a wise, giving, deeply loving daughter and friend.
The chasm that existed between us is now, thankfully,
a meadowland of conversation and love.

DEBBIE REYNOLDS 1932 – 2016

Mothers&Daughters

I have so much I can teach her and pull out of her.
I would say you might encounter defeats but you must never
be defeated. I would teach her to love a lot.
Laugh a lot at the silliest things and be very serious.
I would teach her to love life, I could do that.

MAYA ANGELOU 1928 – 2014

Mothers&Daughters

The most creative and meaningful accomplishment in my life
is to have this daughter who loves, understands and respects me
and gives my life real meaning. Yet, my wish for her
is as old fashioned as can be; health, happiness, peace, love
and a daughter for her as wonderful as she has been for me.

LYNN WILSON SPOHRER

A mother and her daughter grow closer every time they have a successful shopping spree. Shoes off, kettle on, loot divided. It dates back to the Cave…

SAMANTHA ARMSTRONG

Mothers&Daughters

In a rush of nostalgia,
I think back to the time my little girl adored me.
It was all hot hugs, fierce kisses, her face
a warm smudge against my cheek,
her little fingers coiled tightly around my own,
as I rocked her with soft lullabies
in the enclosing darkness.

KATHY LETTE, B. 1958

Mothers&Daughters

The days pass.
The years pass.
And our lives become more interwoven –
Until we see the world
through each other's eyes.

PAM BROWN 1928 – 2014

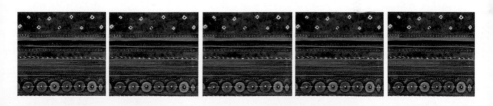

Mothers&Daughters

Thou art thy mother's glass, and she in thee
Calls back the lovely April of her prime.

WILLIAM SHAKESPEARE 1564 – 1616

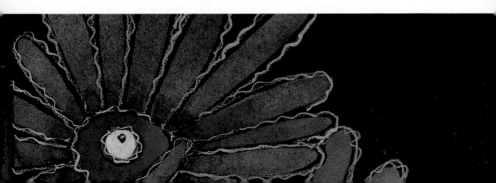

DECEMBER 25

Whether it's a pebble
from the beach
or a diamond necklace,
if the present
is from you
it's sure to be perfect.

LINDA MACFARLANE, B. 1953

JANUARY 8

I would tear down a star and put it into a smart jewelry box if I could. I would seal up love in a long thin bottle so that you could sip it whenever it was needed if I could.

ANNE SEXTON 1928 – 1974

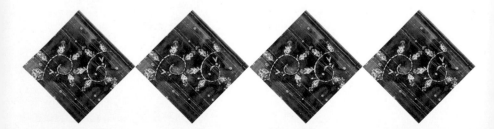

Mothers&Daughters

When she buys me presents like hairbands
and taps and a handwriting book,
it's telling me that she loves me.

NINA ROBERTS, AGE 7

Mothers & Daughters

I have a small daughter called Cleis, who is like a golden flower.
I wouldn't take all Croesus' kingdom with love thrown in, for her.

SAPPHO c.612 – 580 B.C.

DECEMBER 27

Happiness is knowing you are there –
ready to share my joys, to comfort me in sorrow.
You are my companion and my comforter.
And always will be.

PAMELA DUGDALE

Mothers & Daughters

I could sit here and list
all the little things you do for me.
It would take years.
Mostly, I guess you'd just like me
to say that you've made me HAPPY.
Thank you!

HELEN M. EXLEY

Mothers&Daughters

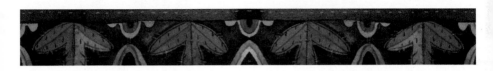

... there is no point trying to pretend
she and I are two separate entities. We're not.
We're complete and utter clones of each other:
the way we speak on the phone,
the way we bolt our food...

MONICA CHONG

Mothers&Daughters

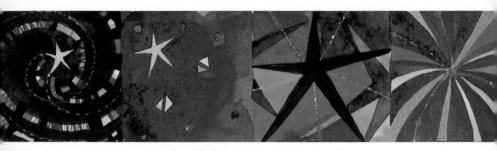

...everything about you, home,
the features, eyes, the hands, your entire form
are the past, present and to come,
the familiarity, the ease
of my living, and my peace.

PAMELA CHALKLEY

DECEMBER 29

Thank you for
making me feel fun,
noticed, important.
What more could I ask!

HELEN M. EXLEY

January 4

Thank you Mother.
It isn't easy to express the things I want to say,
For what goes on unnoticed, every single day.
But still you are there, with all your understanding
And those never-to-be-forgotten words of advice.

JESSE O'NEILL

As we move off into the future, two separate women
each struggling to complete herself, I know
that we will reach out to each other. In my strength
I can be a tree for you to lean against.
In my weakness, I will need your hand.

RITA FREEMAN

Mothers&Daughters

She looked up at me.
Recognition, a memory
of two souls. She relaxed.
The crying stopped.
Her eyes melted through me,
forging a connection in me
with their soft heat. I felt
her love power stir my heart.

SHIRLEY MACLAINE, B. 1934